I0442205

Socio-emotional Impact of Violent Crime

Lynn Langton, Ph.D., and Jennifer Truman, Ph.D., *BJS Statisticians*

In 2009–12, 68% of victims of serious violent crime—rape or sexual assault, robbery, or aggravated assault—reported experiencing socio-emotional problems as a result of their victimization. For this report, socio-emotional problems are defined as the experience of one or more of the following: feelings of moderate to severe distress; significant problems with work or school, such as trouble with a boss, coworkers, or peers; or significant problems with family members or friends, including more arguments than before the victimization, an inability to trust, or not feeling as close after the victimization.

Victims who experienced severe distress as a result of a violent victimization were more likely to report the crime to police and receive victim services than victims with no distress or mild distress (figure 1). About 12% of severely distressed victims reported the crime to police and received victim services compared to 1% of victims with no distress. However, more than a third of victims reporting severe distress and nearly half of those with moderate distress did not report to the police or receive any assistance from victim service providers. In addition, 50% of victims who experienced severe distress and reported to police did not receive victim services. It is not known if they were directed to or offered these services.

FIGURE 1

Violent crime victims who reported the crime to police or received victim services, by level of distress experienced, 2009–2012

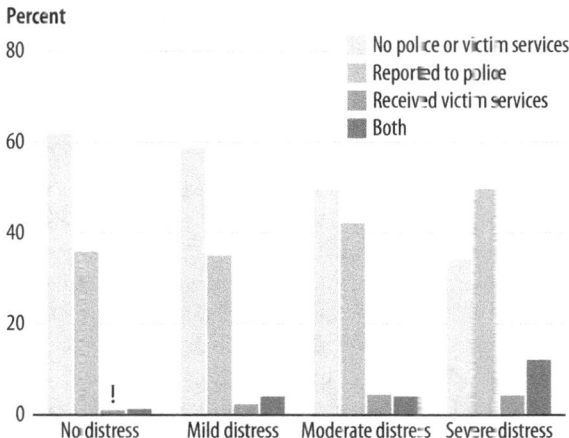

Note: See appendix table 9 for estimates and standard errors. Excludes victimizations in which the level of distress was unknown.

! Interpret with caution. Estimate based on 10 or fewer sample cases, or the coefficient of variation is greater than 50%.

Source: Bureau of Justice Statistics, National Crime Victimization Survey, 2009–2012.

HIGHLIGHTS

This report describes the relationship between violent victimization and the victim's experience of socio-emotional problems, defined as high levels of emotional distress, increased relationship problems, or disruptions at school or work. Data are from the National Crime Victimization Survey.

- Overall, 68% of victims of serious violence experienced socio-emotional problems as a result of their victimization.

- Regardless of the type of violence experienced, a greater percentage of victims of intimate partner violence than stranger violence experienced socio-emotional problems.

- Twelve percent of victims who experienced socio-emotional problems received victim services, compared to 5% of victims reporting no socio-emotional problems.

- More than a third of victims reporting severe distress and nearly half of those with moderate distress did not report to the police or receive any assistance from victim services.

- About three-quarters of victims of rape or sexual assault (75%), robbery (74%), violence involving a firearm (74%), and violence resulting in medical treatment for injuries (77%) experienced socio-emotional problems.

- A greater percentage of female than male victims experienced socio-emotional problems, regardless of the type of violence or victim–offender relationship.

- The majority (91%) of violent crime victims with socio-emotional problems experienced one or more emotional symptoms for a month or more. Most (61%) experienced one or more physical symptoms for a month or more.

This report presents findings on the relationship between the characteristics of violent incidents and victims and the experience of socio-emotional problems. In addition to physical injury and financial loss, victims might experience high levels of emotional distress, increased relationship problems, and significant disruptions and problems at school or work. The report also examines certain help-seeking behaviors of victims suffering from socio-emotional problems as a result of violent victimization.

Data are from the Bureau of Justice Statistics' (BJS) National Crime Victimization Survey (NCVS). The NCVS collects information on nonfatal crimes reported and not reported to police against persons age 12 or older from a nationally representative sample of U.S. households. Questions pertaining to the socio-emotional consequences of victimization were first added to the survey in July 2008. This report aggregates data during the 4-year period from 2009 to 2012, referred to throughout the report as 2009–12. Aggregating data increases the reliability and stability of estimates and facilitates comparisons of detailed victimization characteristics.

Measures of socio-emotional problems

For this report, socio-emotional problems are defined as the experience of moderate to severe distress, problems with work or school, problems in relationships with family or friends, or a combination of the three. (See *Methodology* for wording of the three questions included in the measure of socio-emotional problems.) Although these measures can be examined individually and are presented separately in appendix tables 1, 3, 5, and 7, the three measures are strongly associated (p < .01).

Among violent crime victims who experienced relationship problems or problems with work or school, 80% also reported moderate to severe distress (figure 2). Among those who experienced both relationship and work or school problems, nearly 90% reported feeling moderate to severe distress. Because of the strong relationship between these three variables, for much of the report they are combined and examined as one measure of whether the victim experienced any socio-emotional problems.

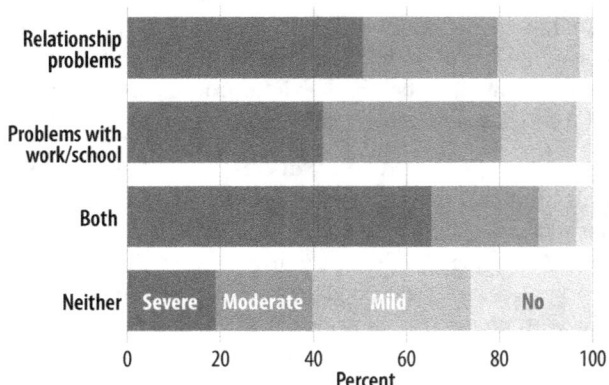

FIGURE 2

Level of distress experienced by violent crime victims, by type of problems experienced as a result of the victimization, 2009–2012

Note: Excludes victimizations in which the level of distress was unknown. See appendix table 10 for estimates and standard errors.

Source: Bureau of Justice Statistics, National Crime Victimization Survey, 2009–2012.

About 70% of rape or sexual assault and robbery
victims experienced moderate to severe distress
resulting from their victimization

In 2009–12, a greater proportion of rape or sexual assault
(71%) and robbery (70%) victims experienced moderate to
severe distress, compared to victims of aggravated (57%)
and simple (46%) assault (figure 3). Among victims of
rape or sexual assault (46%) and robbery (42%), the largest
proportion reported experiencing severe distress. About 1 in
10 rape or sexual assault (11%) and robbery (11%) victims
reported no distress as a result of the victimization. These
incidents include both threats or attempts and completed
crimes. In general, victims of completed crimes experienced
more moderate to severe distress than victims of attempted
or threatened crimes (See appendix table 11).

More serious violent victimizations committed by an
intimate partner (60%) or relative (65%) resulted in
severe distress than those committed by a stranger (31%)

The relationship between the victim and offender is related
to whether a victim experiences socio-emotional problems.
In 2009–12, nearly twice the proportion of victims of serious
violence—rape or sexual assault, robbery, and aggravated
assault—committed by an intimate (60%) and a relative
(65%) indicated that their victimization was severely
distressing, compared to victims of serious violence by a
known offender (36%) and a stranger (31%) (figure 4).
About 17% of serious violence committed by a stranger and
7% of victims of intimate partner violence (IPV) felt no
distress as a result of their victimization.

FIGURE 3

**Level of distress experienced by violent crime victims, by
type of crime, 2009–2012**

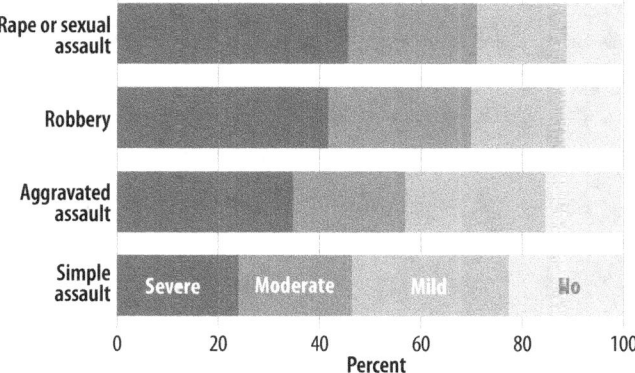

Note: Excludes victimizations in which the level of distress was unknown.
See appendix table 11 for estimates and standard errors.
Source: Bureau of Justice Statistics, National Crime Victimization Survey,
2009–2012.

FIGURE 4

**Level of distress experienced by serious violent crime
victims, by victim–offender relationship, 2009–2012**

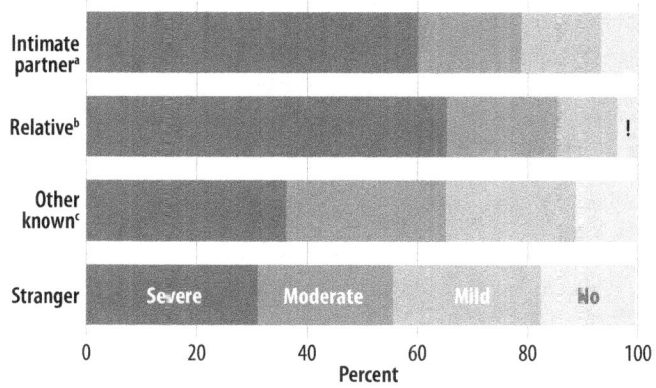

Note: Excludes victimizations in which the level of distress was unknown and the
victim–offender relationship was unknown. See appendix table 12 for estimates
and standard errors.
! Interpret with caution. Based on 10 or fewer sample cases, or the coefficient of
variation is greater than 50%.
[a]Includes victimizations committed by current or former spouses, boyfriends,
and girlfriends.
[b]Includes victimizations committed by family members (excluding intimate
partners).
[c]Includes victimizations committed by close friends or other acquaintances.
Source: Bureau of Justice Statistics, National Crime Victimization Survey,
2009–2012.

Physical and emotional symptoms associated with socio-emotional problems

A victim with socio-emotional problems may experience a range of emotional and physical symptoms. The majority of violent crime victims with socio-emotional problems experienced one or more emotional symptoms (91%) and one or more physical symptoms (61%) for at least a month (table 1). Among all victims of violent crime, the two most widely experienced emotional symptoms were feeling worried or anxious (72%) and feeling angry (70%) for a month or more. The most common physical consequence of experiencing socio-emotional problems was having trouble sleeping for a month or more (47%). Victims of serious violence with socio-emotional problems were more likely to experience one or more emotional and physical symptoms than victims of simple assault with socio-emotional problems.

The percentage of victims who experienced one or more emotional symptoms for at least a month resulting from the socio-emotional problems did not vary with victim–offender relationship. However, a greater percentage of IPV victims (74%) experienced one or more physical symptoms as a result of the socio-emotional problems, compared to victims of violence committed by a known offender (61%) or a stranger (53%). Regardless of the victim–offender relationship, feeling worried or anxious, feeling angry, and having trouble sleeping were among the most common emotional and physical symptoms.

TABLE 1

Physical and emotional symptoms suffered by violent crime victims who experienced socio-emotional problems as a result of the victimization, by type of crime and victim–offender relationship, 2009–2012

	Type of crime			Victim–offender relationship		
Symptom	Total violence	Serious violence	Simple assault	Intimate partner[a]	Other known[b]	Stranger
Emotional	91%	96%	87%	92%	91%	89%
Worried or anxious	72	78	67	79	73	65
Angry	70	76	67	72	72	68
Unsafe	65	73	60	69	63	66
Violated	61	69	56	72	57	57
Vulnerable	60	64	58	69	58	57
Distrustful	56	66	50	60	57	52
Sad or depressed	53	58	50	72	54	37
Other	12	13	12	13	11	14
Physical	61%	67%	57%	74%	61%	53%
Trouble sleeping	47	51	44	61	45	38
Fatigue	34	36	33	52	33	24
Upset stomach	31	32	30	46	29	22
Muscle tension	31	34	28	39	31	25
Headaches	30	37	25	40	31	22
Problems with eating/drinking	27	33	23	43	26	16
High blood pressure	15	16	15	18	17	11
Other	9	12	7	12	8	8

Note: Includes victims who experienced symptoms for a month or more. Victims who did not report experiencing socio-emotional problems (one or more of the following: moderate to severe distress, problems with family or friend releationships, or problems at work or shool) were not asked about physical and emotional symtoms and were excluded from the analysis. Excludes victimizations in which the level of distress was unknown. See appendix table 13 for standard errors.
[a]Includes victimizations committed by current or former spouses, boyfriends, or girlfriends.
[b]Includes victimizations committed by family members (excluding intimate partners), close friends, or other acquaintances.
Source: Bureau of Justice Statistics, National Crime Victimization Survey, 2009–2012.

About 85% of victims of simple assault by an intimate partner experienced socio-emotional problems

For the remainder of this report, victims are characterized as having socio-emotional problems if they experienced one or more of the following: moderate to severe distress, problems with family or friend relationships, or problems at work or school as a result of the victimization. In 2009–12, 57% of all violent crime victims experienced socio-emotional problems as a result of the victimization (table 2). About three-quarters of victims of rape or sexual assault (75%), robbery (74%), violence involving a firearm (74%), and violence resulting in medical treatment for injuries (77%) reported socio-emotional problems. In comparison, about half of victims of simple assault (51%), which does not involve serious physical injuries or a weapon, experienced socio-emotional problems from the victimization.

Across all types of violence, more than 80% of IPV victims reported socio-emotional problems. Regardless of the type of violence, a greater percentage of IPV victims than victims of violence committed by a stranger experienced socio-emotional problems. For instance, about 85% of victims of simple assault committed by an intimate partner experienced socio-emotional problems, compared to 34% of victims of simple assault committed by a stranger. Among the more serious types of violence, a higher percentage of victims of violence committed by a stranger experienced problems than victims of simple assault committed by a stranger. More than 70% of victims of violence committed by a stranger involving a firearm (71%) or resulting in medical treatment for injuries (73%) experienced socio-emotional problems. However, these percentages were still lower than the 88% of IPV victimizations involving a firearm and the 95% of IPV victimizations involving medical treatment for injuries that resulted in socio-emotional problems.

Presence of a weapon or an injury during serious violence was not consistently associated with more socio-emotional problems

A higher percentage of victims of robbery involving both an injury and weapon (85%) experienced socio-emotional problems, compared to victims of robbery that did not involve an injury or weapon (70%) (table 3). However, when the robbery involved a weapon or injury but not both, there was no significant difference in the percentage of victims with socio-emotional problems, compared to victims of robbery involving no weapon or injury.

TABLE 2
Victims who experienced socio-emotional problems as a result of the violent victimization, by type of crime and victim–offender relationship, 2009–2012

Type of violent crime	Total violence	Intimate partner[a]	Other known[b]	Stranger
Total	57%	85%	60%	43%
Serious violence	68%	84%	75%	59%
Rape or sexual assault	75	84	79	67
Robbery	74	82	88	66
Aggravated assault	62	84	66	53
Simple assault	51%	85%	54%	34%
Violence involving a weapon	64%	84%	68%	59%
Firearm	74	88	76	71
Violence involving an injury	71%	88%	72%	59%
Medical treatment received	77	95	77	73

Note: Socio-emotional problems are defined as the experience of one or more of the following: moderate to severe distress, problems with family or friend relationships, or problems at work or school as a result of the victimization. Excludes victimizations in which the level of distress was unknown and the victim–offender relationship was unknown. See appendix table 1 for more detail on the level of distress experienced by type of crime. See appendix table 14 for standard errors.

[a]Includes victimizations committed by current or former spouses, boyfriends, or girlfriends.

[b]Includes victimizations committed by family members (excluding intimate partners), close friends, or other acquaintances.

Source: Bureau of Justice Statistics, National Crime Victimization Survey, 2009–2012.

TABLE 3
Victims who did and did not experience socio-emotional problems as a result of the violent victimization, by type of violent crime, 2009–2012

Type of violent crime	Total	No socio-emotional problems	Socio-emotional problems
Serious	100%	32%	68%
Rape or sexual assault	100%	25	75
With injury	100%	10 !	90
With weapon	100%	41 !	59 !
Both injury and weapon	100%	35 !	65
Without injury or weapon	100%	30	70
Robbery	100%	26	74
With injury	100%	30	70
With weapon	100%	24	76
Both injury and weapon	100%	15	85
Without injury or weapon	100%	30	70
Aggravated assault	100%	38	62
With injury	100%	17	83
With weapon	100%	45	55
Both injury and weapon	100%	31	69
Simple assault	100%	49%	51%

Note: Socio-emotional problems are defined as the experience of one or more of the following: moderate to severe distress, problems with family or friend relationships, or problems at work or school as a result of the victimization. Excludes victimizations in which the level of distress was unknown. See appendix table 15 for standard errors.

! Interpret with caution. Estimate based on 10 or fewer sample cases, or the coefficient of variation is greater than 50%.

Source: Bureau of Justice Statistics, National Crime Victimization Survey, 2009–2012.

This pattern was not consistent for aggravated assault or rape or sexual assault. About 70% of victims of aggravated assault involving both an injury and weapon reported socio-emotional problems. When the aggravated assault involved an injury but not a weapon, 83% of victims experienced socio-emotional problems. Additionally, there was no significant difference in the percentage of victims with socio-emotional problems among those who experienced rape or sexual assault involving both an injury and weapon (65%) or neither an injury nor a weapon (70%).

More victims reported socio-emotional problems when violence occurred at the victim's home than at other locations

Where the violent victimization occurred also affected the likelihood of a victim experiencing socio-emotional problems. Overall, a greater percentage of victims who were victimized at their home (80%) reported socio-emotional problems than victims of violence in other locations (table 4). The relationship between the location of the crime and the experience of socio-emotional problems varied depending on the relationship between the victim and offender. Among victims of violence committed by a stranger, a greater percentage experienced socio-emotional problems when the incident took place at their home (77%), compared to incidents that occurred in other locations (23% to 60%). In comparison, a similar percentage of IPV victims reported socio-emotional problems regardless of whether the violence occurred at the victim's home (87%), at the home of a friend or relative (80%), or in a commercial or public place (88%). Violence in the home was more distressing when the offender was an intimate partner (87%), compared to a stranger (77%). This relationship held for other location types, including at the home of a friend or relative or in a commercial or public place.

TABLE 4

Victims who experienced socio-emotional problems as a result of violent crime victimization, by location of crime and victim–offender relationship, 2009–2012

Location	Total violence	Intimate partner[a]	Other known[b]	Stranger
Total violence	57%	85%	60%	43%
Victim's home or lodging	80	87	73	77
Near victim's home	67	76	70	60
In, at, or near a friend, neighbor, or relative's home	63	80	65	50
Commercial place, parking lot, or other public area	47	88	57	40
School[c]	49	--	53	40
Other location	30	96 !	35	23

Note: Socio-emotional problems are defined as the experience of one or more of the following: moderate to severe distress, problems with family or friend relationships, or problems at work or school as a result of the victimization. Excludes victimizations in which the level of distress was unknown and the victim–offender relationship was unknown. See appendix table 1 for more detail on the level of distress experienced, by location of crime. See appendix table 16 for standard errors.

! Interpret with caution. Estimate based on 10 or fewer sample cases, or the coefficient of variation is greater than 50%.

--Less than 0.5%.

[a]Includes victimizations committed by current or former spouses, boyfriends, or girlfriends.

[b]Includes victimizations committed by family members (excluding intimate partners), close friends, or other acquaintences.

[c]Includes inside a school building or on school property.

Source: Bureau of Justice Statistics, National Crime Victimization Survey, 2009–2012.

12% of victims who experienced socio-emotional problems received assistance from a victim service provider

Experiencing socio-emotional problems may impact whether a victim chooses to seek formal help, such as reporting to police or receiving victim services. While a victim's experience of socio-emotional problems may have been impacted by reporting to police, engaging in the criminal justice system, or seeking victim services, the questions used in this report were intended to capture the response to the victimization rather than to these other sources.

Overall, a greater percentage of victims of violence who experienced socio-emotional problems (54%) reported their victimization to police than victims who did not experience socio-emotional problems (38%) (table 5). This was true for victims of violence committed by other known offenders and strangers. Among IPV victims, a similar percentage who did (60%) and did not (55%) experience socio-emotional problems reported the victimization to police.

A greater percentage of victims of violence who experienced socio-emotional problems (12%) received assistance from victim services than victims who did not experience problems (5%). This relationship held for victims of violence by intimate partners and other known offenders. More than 40% of victims of overall violence (42%) and violence by other known offenders (49%) and strangers (41%) who experienced socio-emotional problems did not report their victimization to the police or receive assistance from victim services.

TABLE 5
Violent crime victims who experienced socio-emotional problems and reported the crime to police or received victim services, by victim–offender relationship, 2009–2012

	Total violence		Intimate partner[a]		Other known[b]		Stranger	
	No socio-emotional problems	Socio-emotional problems	No socio-emotional problems	Socio-emotional problems	No socio-emotional problems	Socio-emotional problems	No socio-emotional problems	Socio-emotional problems
Total violence	100%	100%	100%	100%	100%	100%	100%	100%
Reported to police	38	54	55	60	32	46	40	53
Received victim services	5	12	10	25	7	12	3	4
Neither	61	42	45	32	66	49	58	4

Note: Detail may not sum to total due to a portion of victims who both reported to police and received victim services. Socio-emotional problems are defined as the experience of one or more of the following: moderate to severe distress, problems with family or friend relationships, or problems at work or school as a result of the victimization. Excludes victimizations in which the level of distress was unknown and the victim–offender relationship was unknown. See appendix table 3 for more detail on the level of distress by the types of services received. See appendix table 17 for standard errors.
[a]Includes victimizations committed by current or former spouses, boyfriends, or girlfriends.
[b]Includes victimizations committed by family members (excluding intimate partners), close friends, or other acquaintances.
Source: Bureau of Justice Statistics, National Crime Victimization Survey, 2009–2012.

More females than males experienced socio-emotional problems as a result of their victimization

Regardless of the type of violent crime experienced, a greater percentage of females than males reported socio-emotional problems (table 6). Overall, 72% of female victims of violent crime experienced socio-emotional problems, compared to 44% of male victims. Among victims of serious violence, 79% of females and 58% of males experienced socio-emotional problems.

Marital status appeared to be related to experiences of socio-emotional problems among victims of total violence and serious violence. More victims of all violent crime who were widowed (74%) or divorced or separated (67%) experienced socio-emotional problems than those who were never married (53%) or married (55%). This pattern also held for victims of serious violent crime. However, when marital status was included in a multivariate model controlling for other victim and incident characteristics, the relationship between marital status and socio-emotional problems was no longer significant (see table 10).

The victim's age was associated with the experience of socio-emotional problems for certain types of crime. A greater percentage of all simple assault victims ages 35 to 54 (58%) and 55 or older (63%) experienced socio-emotional problems, compared to victims ages 12 to 17 (45%) and ages 18 to 34 (46%). A similar percentage of serious violence victims ages 12 to 17 (66%), ages 18 to 34 (66%), and ages 35 to 54 (70%) experienced socio-emotional problems.

In general, race or Hispanic origin and education level was not consistently associated with whether a victim experienced socio-emotional problems. A similar percentage of non-Hispanic whites (57%), non-Hispanic blacks (58%), Hispanics (54%), and other races (56%) experienced socio-emotional problems as a result of their violent victimization. Likewise, no differences were detected in the percentage of victims of violence who experienced socio-emotional problems by level of education. For example, 58% of victims of violent crime with an education level of less than high school experienced socio-emotional problems, compared to 57% of victims with a high school or college degree.

TABLE 6
Characteristics of violent crime victims who experienced socio-emotional problems as a result of the victimization, by type of crime, 2009–2012

Victim characteristic	Total violence	Serious violence				Simple assault
		Total	Rape or sexual assault	Robbery	Aggravated assault	
Sex						
Male	44%	58%	49%	69%	52%	36%
Female	72	79	81	81	76	68
Race/Hispanic origin						
White[a]	57%	69%	79%	74%	62%	53%
Black[a]	58	70	68	82	61	49
Hispanic	54	65	61	64	67	48
Other[a,b]	56	64	69 !	71	58	50
Age						
12–17	51%	66%	65%	74%	61%	45%
18–34	53	66	75	72	60	46
35–54	62	70	79	74	65	58
55 or older	66	75	78	79	70	63
Marital status						
Single, never married	53%	66%	70%	70%	61%	46%
Married	55	65	87	71	56	52
Widowed	74	91	# !	92	86 !	64
Divorced or separated	67	77	79	82	72	62
Education						
Less than high school	58%	72%	55%	78%	72%	51%
High school degree or equivalent	57	68	76	75	62	50
College degree	57	67	79	72	60	52

Note: Socio-emotional problems are defined as the experience of one or more of the following: moderate to severe distress, problems with family or friend relationships, or problems at work or school as a result of the victimization. See appendix table 5 for more detail on the level of distress experienced, by victim characteristics. Excludes victimizations in which the level of distress was unknown. See appendix table 18 for standard errors.

\# Rounds to 100%.

! Interpret with caution. Estimate based on 10 or fewer sample cases, or the coefficient of variation is greater than 50%.

[a]Excludes persons of Hispanic or Latino origin.

[b]Includes American Indian, Alaska Native, Hawaiian, Asian, other Pacific Islander, and persons of two or more races.

Source: Bureau of Justice Statistics, National Crime Victimization Survey, 2009–2012.

Whether the offender was an intimate partner, someone else known to the victim, or a stranger, a greater percentage of female than male victims experienced socio-emotional problems as a result of their victimization (table 7). For both males and females, a greater proportion reported socio-emotional problems when the offender was an intimate partner rather than a known offender or stranger.

Older victims were also more likely to experience socio-emotional problems than younger victims, regardless of the victim–offender relationship. In 2009–12, a greater percentage of IPV victims ages 35 to 54 (89%) experienced socio-emotional problems than those ages 18 to 34 (81%). Among victims of violent crime by known offenders, persons ages 35 to 54 (68%) and age 55 or older (75%) experienced more socio-emotional problems than persons ages 12 to 17 (55%) and ages 18 to 34 (54%). For victims of violent crime by strangers, a greater percentage of victims age 55 or older (53%) experienced socio-emotional problems than victims ages 12 to 17 (41%) and ages 18 to 34 (41%).

Marital status appeared to be related to experiencing socio-emotional problems among victims of violence by intimate partners and other known offenders. For instance, more victims of IPV who were divorced or separated (89%) experienced socio-emotional problems as a result of their victimization than victims who were never married (81%). However, when marital status was included in a multivariate model controlling for other victim and incident characteristics, victim-offender relationship was significantly related to socio-emotional problems while marital status was not (see table 10).

The proportion of victims who experienced socio-emotional problems also varied by level of education among IPV victims. A greater percentage of IPV victims with a college education experienced socio-emotional problems (88%) than IPV victims with a high school education (79%). Among victims of violence committed by a stranger, a slightly greater percentage of victims with less than a high school education (50%) experienced socio-emotional problems than those with a college education (41%). However, similar percentages of victims of violence by other known offenders experienced socio-emotional problems, regardless of their level of education.

Regardless of the relationship between victim and offender, the proportion of violent crime victims who experienced socio-emotional problems did not vary by the race or Hispanic origin of the victim. Among IPV victims, whites (87%), blacks (80%), and other races (86%) experienced similar proportions of socio-emotional problems. Victims of violent crime by other known offenders experienced similar amounts of socio-emotional problems, regardless of their race or Hispanic origin.

TABLE 7
Characteristics of violent crime victims who experienced socio-emotional problems as a result of the victimization, by victim–offender relationship, 2009–2012

Victim characteristic	Intimate partner[a]	Other known[b]	Stranger
Sex			
Male	70%	51%	35%
Female	88	69	61
Race/Hispanic origin			
White[c]	87%	61%	41%
Black[c]	80	59	49
Hispanic	73	62	44
Other[c,d]	86	58	47
Age			
12–17	#!	55%	41%
18–34	81%	54	41
35–54	89	68	44
55 or older	90	75	53
Marital status			
Single, never married	81%	56%	43%
Married	80	66	42
Widowed	#!	86	38
Divorced or separated	89	64	47
Education			
Less than high school	#	58%	50%
High school degree or equivalent	79%	59	45
College degree	88	63	41

Note: Socio-emotional problems are defined as the experience of one or more of the following: moderate to severe distress, problems with family or friend relationships, or problems at work or school as a result of the victimization. Excludes victimizations in which the level of distress was unknown and the victim–offender relationship was unknown. See appendix table 19 for standard errors.

Rounds to 100%.

! Interpret with caution. Estimate based on 10 or fewer sample cases, or the coefficient of variation is greater than 50%.

[a]Includes victimizations committed by current or former spouses, boyfriends, or girlfriends.

[b]Includes victimizations committed by family members (excluding intimate partners), close friends, or other acquaintances.

[c]Excludes persons of Hispanic or Latino origin.

[d]Includes American Indian, Alaska Native, Hawaiian, Asian, other Pacific Islander, and persons of two or more races.

Source: Bureau of Justice Statistics, National Crime Victimization Survey, 2009–2012.

Victims who lived in households headed by a single female experienced more socio-emotional problems than victims living in other households

Characteristics such as household composition, income, and location of residence may be related to a victim experiencing socio-emotional problems. A greater percentage of victims of violent crime who lived in households headed by a single female with (67%) and without children (79%) experienced socio-emotional problems than those who lived in households headed by a single male with (47%) and without children (45%) (table 8). This relationship also held true for victims of both serious violence and simple assault. Households headed by married adults with (53%) and without children (56%) experienced similar proportions of socio-emotional problems as a result of their violent victimization. The same occurred for victims of both serious violence and simple assault.

For victims of serious violent crime, a greater percentage of persons with an income of $24,999 or less experienced socio-emotional problems (72%) than persons with an income of $75,000 or more (58%). Among victims of simple assault, a greater percentage of persons with an income of $24,999 or less experienced socio-emotional problems (60%) than those with greater incomes (45% to 52%).

Generally, no statistical differences were detected by location of residence as to whether victims of violent crime experienced socio-emotional problems. A similar percentage of persons living in urban areas (57%) experienced socio-emotional problems, compared to those living in suburban areas (56%) and those living in rural areas (62%). However, a smaller percentage of victims of simple assault living in urban (50%) and suburban (50%) areas experienced socio-emotional problems than victims living in rural areas (59%).

TABLE 8
Household characteristics of violent crime victims who experienced socio-emotional problems as a result of the victimization, by type of crime, 2009–2012

Household characteristic	Total violence	Serious violence				Simple assault
		Total	Rape or sexual assault	Robbery	Aggravated assault	
Composition						
Single male						
No children	45%	58%	19%!	67%	58%	38%
With children	47	54	59!	#!	31!	44
Single female						
No children	79	81	85	92	69	62
With children	67	78	87	83	72	79
Married[a]						
No children	56	68	87	68	61	51
With children	53	62	68	70	58	50
Other[b]	55	67	75	70	63	48
Income						
$24,999 or less	65%	72%	65%	80%	67%	60%
$25,000–49,999	54	65	80	71	60	48
$50,000–74,999	52	67	82	68	53	45
$75,000 or more	49	58	83	57	53	45
Unknown	58	73	75	76	69	52
Location of residence						
Urban	57%	69%	76%	74%	63%	50%
Suburban	56	67	78	72	59	50
Rural	62	69	60	79	68	59

Note: Socio-emotional problems are defined as the experience of one or more of the following: moderate to severe distress, problems with family or friend relationships, or problems at work or school as a result of the victimization. Excludes victimizations in which the level of distress was unknown. See appendix table 7 for more detail on the level of distress, by household characteristics. See appendix table 20 for standard errors.

Rounds to 100%.

! Interpret with caution. Estimate based on 10 or fewer sample cases, or the coefficient of variation is greater than 50%.

[a]Includes a married couple living with no other adults.

[b]Includes both single and married adults living with other adults (relatives or nonrelatives), both with and without children.

Source: Bureau of Justice Statistics, National Crime Victimization Survey, 2009–2012.

About 9 in 10 IPV victims who lived in households headed by single females experienced socio-emotional problems

A similar percentage of victims of IPV who lived in households headed by single females both with (87%) and without children (94%) and by single males with children (95%) experienced socio-emotional problems (table 9). These percentages were greater than IPV victims who lived in households headed by single males without children (66%). IPV victims who lived in households headed by married adults with no children (91%) experienced a greater percentage of socio-emotional problems than those who lived in households with children (70%). For victims of violent crime by a known offender, a greater percentage of persons who lived in households headed by a single female without children (75%) experienced socio-emotional problems than those living in households headed by a single male without children (52%). Households headed by married adults without children (69%) experienced more socio-emotional problems than those with children (57%) when the violent victimization was committed by a known offender. Among victims of violence by strangers, persons who lived in households headed by single females experienced greater socio-emotional problems than households headed by males.

Income was associated with the experience of socio-emotional problems among IPV victims, and violence by other known offenders and strangers. IPV victims who had an income of $75,000 or more experienced more socio-emotional problems (96%), compared to IPV victims in other income brackets. For victims of violent crime by a known offender, a greater percentage of persons with an income of $24,999 or less experienced socio-emotional problems (65%) than persons with an income of $75,000 or more (52%). Among victims of violent crime by a stranger, a greater percentage of persons with an income of $24,999 or less experienced socio-emotional problems (55%) than those with greater incomes.

In general, no differences were detected in the proportion of victims who experienced socio-emotional problems by victim–offender relationship and location of residence. A similar percentage of IPV victims living in urban areas experienced socio-emotional problems (83%), compared to those living in suburban (86%) and rural areas (85%). As with IPV, victims of violence by other known offenders experienced similar proportions of socio-emotional problems, regardless of their location of residence. However, among victims of violence by strangers, a smaller percentage of victims living in suburban areas (39%) experienced socio-emotional problems than victims in rural areas (51%).

TABLE 9
Household characteristics of violent crime victims who experienced socio-emotional problems as a result of the victimization, by victim–offender relationship, 2009–2012

Household characteristic	Intimate partner[a]	Other known[b]	Stranger
Composition			
Single male			
No children	66%	52%	38%
With children	95	33 !	37 !
Single female			
No children	94	75	76
With children	87	59	56
Married[c]			
No children	91	69	39
With children	70	57	46
Other[d]	85	61	39
Income			
$24,999 or less	84%	65%	55%
$25,000–49,999	83	62	38
$50,000–74,999	84	59	40
$75,000 or more	96	52	35
Unknown	82	59	46
Location of residence			
Urban	83%	59%	46%
Suburban	86	62	39
Rural	85	59	51

Note: Socio-emotional problems are defined as the experience of one or more of the following: moderate to severe distress, problems with family or friend relationships, or problems at work or school as a result of the victimization. Excludes victimizations in which the level of distress was unknown and the victim–offender relationship was unknown. See appendix table 21 for standard errors.

! Interpret with caution. Estimate based on 10 or fewer sample cases, or the coefficient of variation is greater than 50%.

[a]Includes victimizations committed by current or former spouses, boyfriends, or girlfriends.

[b]Includes victimizations committed by family members (excluding intimate partners), close friends, or other acquaintances.

[c]Includes a married couple living with no other adults.

[d]Includes both single and married adults living with other adults (relatives or nonrelatives), both with and without children.

Source: Bureau of Justice Statistics, National Crime Victimization Survey, 2009–2012.

After controlling for other variables, IPV victims were five times more likely to experience socio-emotional problems than victims of violence by strangers

To assess the unique contribution of incident and victim characteristics to the probability of experiencing socio-emotional problems, a logistic regression analysis was used. The analysis produced estimates of the association between each independent variable (the victim and incident characteristics) and the dependent variable (the likelihood of experiencing socio-emotional problems) after accounting for other variables in the model. See *Methodology* for more information about logistic regression techniques.

In general, the logistic regression analysis revealed similar patterns in the probability of a victim experiencing socio-emotional problems as shown in the tables discussed in this report. Among the variables examined, the victim–offender relationship—specifically victimization by an intimate partner—had the greatest relative impact on the likelihood of experiencing socio-emotional problems (table 10). IPV victims were more than five times more likely to experience socio-emotional problems than victims of violence committed by a stranger (odds ratio 5.4). Victims of violence by other known offenders were two times more likely to experience socio-emotional problems than victims of violence committed by a stranger (2.0).

Characteristics of the violent incident also had an impact on the likelihood of experiencing socio-emotional problems. Victims of robbery were 2.7 times more likely to experience socio-emotional problems than victims of simple assault. Victims who suffered an injury during the victimization were two times more likely to experience socio-emotional problems than victims who were not injured. When a weapon was present, victims were 1.7 times more likely to experience socio-emotional problems than when a weapon was not involved.

After accounting for characteristics of the incident and victim–offender relationship, certain victim characteristics were also still related to the experience of socio-emotional problems. Female victims were about 2.6 times more likely than males to experience socio-emotional problems. Victims ages 35 to 54 (1.5) and age 55 or older (2.1) were significantly more likely than victims ages 12 to 17 to experience socio-emotional problems. Other characteristics, such as race, marital status, and education, had little independent impact on the probability of experiencing socio-emotional problems.

TABLE 10
Logistic regression analysis of the effect of victim characteristics, type of crime, and victim–offender relationship on the probability of victims experiencing socio-emotional problems, 2009–2012

	Odds ratio[a]	
	First model	Final model
Victim characteristic		
Female[b]	2.5†	2.6†
Black[c]	0.8	~
Other race[c]	1.0	~
Hispanic[c]	0.9	~
Ages 18–34[d]	0.9	~
Ages 35–54[d]	1.5†	1.5†
Age 55 or older[d]	1.9†	2.1†
Married[e]	1.0	~
Widowed[e]	1.1	~
Divorced or separated[e]	1.0	~
Less than high school degree[f]	1.5	~
High school degree or equivalent[f]	0.9	~
Type of crime		
Rape or sexual assault[g]	1.8†	~
Robbery[g]	3.3†	2.7†
Aggravated assault[g]	1.5	~
Victim–offender relationship		
Intimate partner[h]	5.9†	5.4†
Other known[h]	2.0†	2.0†
Incident characteristics		
Series victimization[i]	0.8	~
Injury[j]	1.8†	2.0†
Weapon present[k]	1.2	1.7†
Do not know if weapon present[k]	1.7†	1.7†

Note: Socio-emotional problems are defined as the experience of one or more of the following: moderate to severe distress, problems with family or friend relationships, or problems at work or school as a result of the victimization. Estimates represent the probability of that a victim with a particular characteristic has experienced socio-emotional problems conditional on the victim having the mean value for all other predictors in the model. See appendix table 22 for coefficients and standard errors.
†Significant at 95%.
~Characteristics deleted from model when Wald statistic was not significant at the 95%-confidence level.
[a]An odds ratio greater than 1 indicates that the variable is associated with an increased likelihood that the victim experienced socio-emotional problems. Variables with larger odds ratios have a larger effect on the probability of experiencing socio-emotional problems than variables with smaller odds ratios.
[b]Compared to males.
[c]Compared to whites.
[d]Compared to ages 12 to 17.
[e]Compared to never married.
[f]Compared to college education.
[g]Compared to simple assault.
[h]Compared to stranger.
[i]Compared to nonseries victimization. High frequency repeat victimizations (or series victimizations) are six or more similar but separate victimizations that occur with such frequency that the victim is unable to recall each individual event or describe each event in detail.
[j]Compared to no injury.
[k]Compared to no weapon present.
Source: Bureau of Justice Statistics, National Crime Victimization Survey, 2009–2012.

Methodology

Survey coverage

The National Crime Victimization Survey (NCVS) is an annual data collection conducted by the U.S. Census Bureau for the Bureau of Justice Statistics (BJS). The NCVS is a self-report survey in which interviewed persons are asked about the number and characteristics of victimizations experienced during the prior 6 months. It collects information on nonfatal personal crimes (rape or sexual assault, robbery, aggravated and simple assault, and personal larceny) and household property crimes (burglary, motor vehicle theft, and other theft) both reported and not reported to police.

In addition to providing annual level and change estimates on criminal victimization, the NCVS is the primary source of information on the nature of criminal victimization incidents. Survey respondents provide information about themselves (e.g., age, sex, race and Hispanic origin, marital status, education level, and income) and whether they experienced a victimization. For each victimization incident, the NCVS collects information about the offender (e.g., age, race and Hispanic origin, sex, and victim–offender relationship), characteristics of the crime (including time and place of occurrence, use of weapons, nature of injury, and economic consequences), whether the crime was reported to police, reasons the crime was or was not reported, and victims' experiences with the criminal justice system.

The NCVS is administered to persons age 12 or older from a nationally representative sample of households in the United States. The NCVS defines a household as a group of members who all reside at a sampled address. Persons are considered household members when the sampled address is their usual place of residence at the time of the interview and when they have no usual place of residence elsewhere. Once selected, households remain in the sample for 3 years, and eligible persons in these households are interviewed every 6 months either in person or over the phone for a total of seven interviews. Generally, all first interviews are conducted in person. New households rotate into the sample on an ongoing basis to replace outgoing households that have been in sample for the 3-year period. The sample includes persons living in group quarters such as dormitories, rooming houses, and religious group dwellings, and excludes persons living in military barracks and institutional settings such as correctional or hospital facilities, and individuals who are homeless.

Nonresponse and weighting adjustments

In 2012, 92,390 households and 162,940 persons age 12 or older were interviewed for the NCVS. Each household was interviewed twice during the year. The response rate was 87% for households and 87% for eligible persons. Victimizations that occurred outside of the United States were excluded from this report. In 2012, less than 1% of the unweighted victimizations occurred outside of the United States and were excluded from the analyses. Estimates in this report use data from the 1993 to 2012 NCVS data files, weighted to produce annual estimates of victimization for persons age 12 or older living in U.S. households. Since the NCVS relies on a sample rather than a census of the entire U.S. population, weights are designed to inflate sample point estimates to known population totals and to compensate for survey nonresponse and other aspects of the sample design.

NCVS data files include both person and household weights. Person weights provide an estimate of the population represented by each person in the sample. Household weights provide an estimate of the U.S. household population represented by each household in the sample. After proper adjustment, both household and person weights are also typically used to form the denominator in calculations of crime rates.

Victimization weights used in this analysis account for the number of persons present during an incident and for high frequency repeat victimizations (or series victimizations). Series victimizations are similar in type but occur with such frequency that a victim is unable to recall each individual event or describe each event in detail. Survey procedures allow NCVS interviewers to identify and classify these similar victimizations as series victimizations and to collect detailed information on only the most recent incident in the series. The weight counts series incidents as the actual number of incidents reported by the victim, up to a maximum of 10 incidents. Including series victimizations in national rates results in large increases in the level of violent victimization; however, trends in violence are generally similar regardless of whether series victimizations are included. In 2012, series incidents accounted for about 1% of all victimizations and 4% of all violent victimizations. Weighting series incidents as the number of incidents up to a maximum of 10 incidents produces more reliable estimates of crime levels, while the cap at 10 minimizes the effect of extreme outliers on the rates. Additional information on the series enumeration is provided in the report *Methods for Counting High Frequency Repeat Victimizations in the National Crime Victimization Survey* (NCJ 237308, BJS web, April 2012).

Items used to measure socio-emotional problems

For this report, three NCVS questions were used as a measure of socio-emotional problems. Socio-emotional problems were defined as the experience of one or more of the following: feelings of moderate to severe distress; significant problems with work or school, such as trouble with a boss, coworkers, or peers; or significant problems with family members or friends, including more arguments than before the victimization, an inability to trust, or not feeling as close after the victimization. The specific NCVS questions that went into this measure were:

- Being a victim of crime affects people in different ways. Next I would like to ask you some questions about how being a crime victim may have affected you. Did being a victim of this crime lead you to have significant problems with your job or schoolwork, or trouble with your boss, coworkers, or peers?

- Did being a victim of this crime lead you to have significant problems with family members or friends, including getting into more arguments or fights than you did before, not feeling you could trust them as much, or not feeling as close to them as you did before?

- How distressing was being a victim of this crime to you? Was it not at all distressing, mildly distressing, moderately distressing, or severely distressing?

Item nonresponse on questions about socio-emotional problems

In 2009–12, about 14% of violent crime victims were not administered the questions related to socio-emotional problems and were excluded from the report analyses. These victimizations were originally classified as property crimes, which are eliminated from the section on socio-emotional problems by design, but were later reclassified as violent victimizations when it became apparent that the victim was present during the incident. A comparison of the characteristics of violent crime victims who were and were not administered the socio-emotional problems questions was conducted to assess whether significant differences exist between the two groups (table 11).

Although there were some differences between the groups, the analysis did not show evidence that inclusion of the victims who did not receive the questions would significantly impact the findings. Among the differences identified, a greater percentage of victims excluded from the analysis were black (21%) and from suburban areas (54%), compared to victims who were included in the analysis. There also

appeared to be variations in the victim–offender relationship and income distributions, but these were due to differences in the percentage of unknown information between the two groups. Unless all members of the excluded group responded to the questions in the same way—a highly improbably scenario—the within group patterns of distress would not change significantly.

TABLE 11

Characteristics of incidents and victims who were and were not administered NCVS distress questions, 2009–2012

Characteristic	Distress questions not administered	Distress questions administered
Type of violence	100%	100%
Rape or sexual assault	2	5†
Robbery	10	11
Aggravated assault	17	17
Simple assault	71	67
Victim–offender relationship		
Intimate partner	10%	16% †
Relative	3	8†
Other known	27	32‡
Stranger	21	41†
Unknown	38	3†
Sex		
Male	51%	53%
Female	49	47
Race/Hispanic origin		
White[a]	59%	65% ‡
Black[a]	21	15†
Hispanic	14	14
Other[a,b]	5	6
Age		
12–17	17%	17%
18–34	43	42
35–54	32	31
55 or older	9	11
Income		
$24,999 or less	18%	28% †
$25,000–49,999	20	19
$50,000–74,999	14	12
$75,000 or more	16	17
Unknown	32	24†
Location of residence		
Urban	32%	42% †
Suburban	54	45†
Rural	15	14

Note: See appendix table 23 for standard errors.
† Indicates the difference between groups was significant at p <.05.
‡ Indicates the difference between groups was significant at p <.1.
[a]Excludes persons of Hispanic or Latino origin.
[b]Includes American Indian, Alaska Native, Hawaiian, Asian, other Pacific Islander, and persons of two or more races.
Source: Bureau of Justice Statistics, National Crime Victimization Survey, 2009–2012.

Standard error computations

When national estimates are derived from a sample, as with the NCVS, caution must be used when comparing one estimate to another or when comparing estimates over time. Although one estimate may be larger than another, estimates based on a sample have some degree of sampling error. The sampling error of an estimate depends on several factors, including the amount of variation in the responses and the size of the sample. When the sampling error around an estimate is taken into account, the estimates that appear different may not be statistically different.

One measure of the sampling error associated with an estimate is the standard error. The standard error can vary from one estimate to the next. Generally, an estimate with a small standard error provides a more reliable approximation of the true value than an estimate with a large standard error. Estimates with relatively large standard errors are associated with less precision and reliability and should be interpreted with caution.

To generate standard errors around numbers and estimates from the NCVS, the Census Bureau produced generalized variance function (GVF) parameters for BJS. GVFs account for aspects of the NCVS complex sample design and represent the curve fitted to a selection of individual standard errors based on the Jackknife Repeated Replication technique. The GVF parameters were used to generate standard errors for each point estimate (such as counts, percentages, and rates) in this report.

BJS conducted tests to determine whether differences in estimated numbers and percentages in this report were statistically significant once sampling error was taken into account. Using statistical programs developed specifically for the NCVS, all comparisons in the text were tested for significance. Student's t-statistic was the primary test procedure, which tests the difference between two sample estimates.

Data users can use the estimates and the standard errors of the estimates provided in this report to generate a confidence interval around the estimate as a measure of the margin of error. The following example illustrates how standard errors can be used to generate confidence intervals:

In 2009–12, according to the NCVS, 57% of victims of violent crime experienced socio-emotional problems as a result of the victimization (see table 2). Using GVFs, it was determined that the estimated percentage has a standard error of 1.6 (see appendix table 14). A confidence interval around the estimate was generated by multiplying the standard errors by ±1.96 (the t-score of a normal, two-tailed distribution that excludes 2.5% at either end of the distribution). Therefore, the 95% confidence interval around the 57% estimate from 2012 is 57 ± (1.6 X 1.96) or (54 to 60).

In others words, if different samples using the same procedures were taken from the U.S. population in 2009–12, 95% of the time 54% to 60% of all violent victims would report experiencing socio-emotional problems. In this report, BJS also calculated a coefficient of variation (CV) for all estimates, representing the ratio of the standard error to the estimate. CVs provide a measure of reliability and a means for comparing the precision of estimates across measures with differing levels or metrics. In cases where the CV was greater than 50%, or the unweighted sample had 10 or fewer cases, the estimate was noted with a "!" symbol. (Interpret data with caution. Estimate based on 10 or fewer sample cases, or the coefficient of variation is greater than 50%.)

Impact of interview recency on level of distress

The time elapsed from the victimization to the NCVS interview may be associated with the level of distress that a victim reported. To examine this, the distribution of level of distress was examined for victimizations that occurred less than 1 month to 5 months or more prior to the interview. The level of distress reported by victims did not appear to be related to the recency of the interview (figure 5). A similar percentage of victims of violent incidents reported moderate to severe distress regardless of the number of months from the victimization to the interview. For example, 26% of victims who were interviewed less than 1 month after their victimization reported severe distress, compared to 28% of victims who were interviewed 5 months after their victimization.

FIGURE 5

Recency of interview, by level of distress reported, 2009–2012

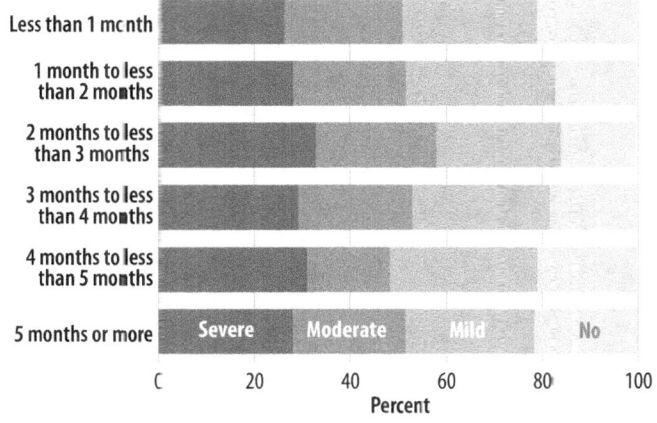

Note: See appendix table 24 for estimates and standard errors.

Source: Bureau of Justice Statistics, National Crime Victimization Survey, 2009–2012.

Logistic regression statistical techniques

The analyses conducted in table 10 employed the technique of logistic regression for categorical binary outcomes, which produces coefficients estimating the relationship between independent variables on the probability of the dependent outcome. In this case, logistic regression was used to determine what characteristics are statistically significant for predicting a dichotomous outcome, a victim experiencing socio-emotional problems or not experiencing socio-emotional problems, and if these relationships persist after controlling for other characteristics. The selected victim and incident characteristics examined were sex, race and Hispanic origin, age, marital status, education level, type of crime (e.g., serious violence or simple assault), and victim–offender relationship. A logistic model was iteratively run under a backwards selection technique until only predictors that were significant at the 95% level of confidence remained.

The coefficients produced were transformed into an odds ratio to show the effect of a change in a given independent variable. The odds ratio compared whether the probability that a victim experienced socio-emotional problems was the same for two groups (e.g. males and females) conditional on the victim having the mean value of all other predictors in the model. The formula for calculating an odds ratio is—

$$exp\ (B)$$

where *exp* equals the base of the natural logarithm e (a constant equal to 2.71828) and *B* equals the logistic regression coefficient for a given independent variable. An odds ratio greater than 1 indicates that the characteristic is associated with an increased likelihood that the victim experienced socio-emotional problems. Characteristics with larger odds ratios have a larger effect on the probability of experiencing socio-emotional problems than characteristics with smaller odds ratios. For example, in appendix table 22, the coefficient for serious violence is 0.9. The exponentiated logistic regression coefficient of 0.9 produces an odds ratio of 2.5. The odds ratio of 2.5 for serious violence is the ratio of the odds of victims of serious violence experiencing socio-emotional problems to the odds of a victim of simple assault (the reference or comparison group), after accounting for the effect of all of the other predictor variables in the model. That is, the odds ratio of 2.5 indicates that the odds of a victim of serious violence experiencing socio-emotional problems is 2.5 times higher than a victim of simple assault (the comparison group).

The logistic regression analyses were conducted with SPSS Complex Samples using weighted data and accounting for the NCVS complex sample design. Prior to conducting the regression analyses, all variables were tested to ensure that multicollinearity was not a problem for the models. The variances and standard errors were then computed using the Taylor Series Linearization method. Wald F-statistics were calculated to test for statistical significance of the effects of each victim and incident characteristic. The Wald F-statistics were used to test the null hypothesis that all regression coefficients are equal to zero for each characteristics (i.e., the probability of experiencing socio-emotional problems is the same across all categories of the selected characteristics), conditional on all other victim or incident characteristics being including in the model.

APPENDIX TABLE 1

Level of distress, relationship problems, and school or work problems experienced by violent crime victims, by type of crime and incident characteristics, 2009–2012

Type of violent crime	Total	Distress				Family/friend relationship problems[a]	Work/school problems[b]
		No	Mild	Moderate	Severe		
Total	100%	19%	28%	23%	29%	21%	18%
Serious violence	100%	13%	23%	25%	39%	25%	23%
Rape or sexual assault	100	11	18	26	46	37	38
Robbery	100	11	19	28	42	30	20
Aggravated assault	100	15	28	22	35	18	19
Simple assault	100%	22%	31%	22%	24%	19%	15%
Domestic violence[c]	100%	6%	18%	23%	53%	45%	26%
Intimate partner violence[d]	100	5	14	25	56	44	31
Stranger violence	100%	28%	31%	21%	19%	8%	10%
Violence involving a weapon	100%	15%	26%	22%	37%	21%	20%
Firearm	100	9	22	24	44	25	23
Violence involving an injury	100%	12%	22%	24%	42%	28%	23%
Formal medical treatment received	100	9	18	24	49	32	27
Location of victimization							
Victim's home or lodging	100%	7%	19%	21%	52%	42%	23%
Near victim's home	100	14	23	23	40	21	16
In, at, or near a friend, neighbor, or relative's home	100	17	29	24	29	29	16
Commercial place, parking lot, or other public area	100	27	29	23	21	11	13
School[d]	100	19	39	31	10	18	23
Other location	100	32	41	17	10	7	10

Note: See appendix table 2 for standard errors.

[a]Includes victims reporting significant problems with family members or friends, including getting into more arguments or fights than before, not feeling able to trust them as much, or not feeling as close to them as before the crime.

[b]Includes victims reporting significant problems with job or school, such as trouble with a boss, coworker, or peer.

[c]Includes victimization committed by intimate partners (current or former spouses, boyfriends, or girlfriends) and family members.

[d]Includes victimization committed by current or former spouses, boyfriends, or girlfriends.

Source: Bureau of Justice Statistics, National Crime Victimization Survey, 2009–2012.

APPENDIX TABLE 2

Standard errors for appendix table 1: Level of distress, relationship problems, and school or work problems experienced by violent crime victims, by type of crime and incident characteristics, 2009–2012

Type of violent crime	Distress				Family/friend relationship problems	Work/school problems
	No	Mild	Moderate	Severe		
Total	1.1%	1.3%	1.2%	1.3%	1.1%	1.0%
Serious violence	1.3%	1.7%	1.7%	2.0%	1.7%	1.7%
Rape or sexual assault	2.2	2.7	3.2	3.8	3.7	3.7
Robbery	1.7	2.3	2.7	3.1	2.8	2.4
Aggravated assault	1.7	2.3	2.1	2.5	1.9	1.9
Simple assault	1.3%	1.5%	1.3%	1.3%	1.2%	1.0%
Domestic violence	1.4%	2.5%	2.9%	3.6%	3.6%	3.0%
Intimate partner violence	1.0	1.7	2.3	2.8	2.7	2.5
Stranger violence	1.7%	1.8%	1.5%	1.4%	0.9%	1.0%
Violence involving a weapon	1.6%	2.1%	1.9%	2.4%	1.9%	1.9%
Firearm	1.9	2.9	3.0	3.7	3.1	3.0
Violence involving an injury	1.3%	1.8%	1.8%	2.2%	2.0%	1.8%
Formal medical treatment received	1.5	2.1	2.4	3.0	2.7	2.6
Location of victimization						
Victim's home or lodging	1.0%	1.8%	1.9%	2.5%	2.4%	1.9%
Near victim's home	1.7	2.2	2.2	2.7	2.1	1.8
In, at, or near a friend, neighbor, or relative's home	2.4	3.1	2.8	3.1	3.1	2.4
Commercial place, parking lot, or other public area	1.8	1.9	1.7	1.6	1.2	1.4
School	2.2	2.9	2.7	1.6	2.1	2.4
Other location	2.9	3.1	2.2	1.6	1.3	1.6

Source: Bureau of Justice Statistics, National Crime Victimization Survey, 2009–2012.

APPENDIX TABLE 3

Level of distress, relationship problems, and school or work problems experienced by violent crime victims, by whether victim reported to police or received victim services, 2009–2012

Help-seeking behavior	Total	Distress				Family/friend relationship problems[a]	Work/school problems[b]
		No	Mild	Moderate	Severe		
Total	100%	19%	28%	23%	29%	21%	18%
Reported to police	100%	17	24	24	35	20	17
Received victim services	100%	6!	21	33	40	44	33
Both	100%	4	20	16	60	44	32
Neither	100%	24	33	23	20	18	15

Note: Details may not sum to total due to missing responses. See appendix table 4 for standard errors.

[a]Includes victims reporting significant problems with family members or friends, including getting into more arguments or fights than before, not feeling able to trust them as much, or not feeling as close to them as before the crime.

[b]Includes victims reporting significant problems with job or school, such as trouble with a boss, coworker, or peer.

Source: Bureau of Justice Statistics, National Crime Victimization Survey, 2009–2012.

APPENDIX TABLE 4

Standard errors for appendix table 3: Level of distress, relationship problems, and school or work problems experienced by violent crime victims, by whether victim reported to police or received victim services, 2009–2012

Help-seeking behavior	Distress				Family/friend relationship problems	Work/school problems
	No	Mild	Moderate	Severe		
Total	1.1%	1.3%	1.2%	1.3%	1.1%	1.0%
Reported to police	1.3	1.6	1.6	1.9	1.5	1.3
Received victim services	2.2!	3.9	4.6	4.9	5.0	4.6
Both	1.3	2.9	2.7	4.0	3.9	3.6
Neither	1.5	1.7	1.5	1.4	1.3	1.2

Source: Bureau of Justice Statistics, National Crime Victimization Survey, 2009–2012.

Level of distress, relationship problems, and school or work problems experienced by violent crime victims, by victim characteristics, 2009–2012

Victim characteristic	Total	Distress				Family/friend relationship problems[a]	Work/school problems[b]
		No	Mild	Moderate	Severe		
Sex							
Male	100%	29%	32%	20%	18%	13%	12%
Female	100%	8	24	26	41	30	24
Race/Hispanic origin							
White	100%	19%	28%	24%	29%	22%	13%
Black	100%	20	27	21	31	23	15
Hispanic	100%	20	32	21	27	18	13
Other	100%	24	26	20	30	22	20
Age							
12–17	100%	21%	36%	27%	16%	19%	23%
18–34	100%	21	31	22	26	21	17
35–54	100%	17	23	22	37	23	16
55 or older	100%	15	22	26	37	21	12
Marital status							
Single, never married	100%	20%	33%	24%	23%	20%	18%
Married	100%	20	28	26	25	18	11
Widowed	100%	14 !	13	18	55	29	24
Divorced or separated	100%	18	19	19	45	28	22
Education							
Less than high school	100%	18%	33%	30%	18%	22%	26%
High school degree or equivalent	100%	19	28	21	31	22	16
College degree	100%	20	27	23	30	21	16

Note: See appendix table 6 for standard errors.

! Interpret with caution. Estimate based on 10 or fewer sample cases, or the coefficient of variation is greater than 50%.

[a]Includes victims reporting significant problems with family members or friends, including getting into more arguments or fights than before, not feeling able to trust them as much, or not feeling as close to them as before the crime.

[b]Includes victims reporting significant problems with job or school, such as trouble with a boss, coworker, or peer.

Source: Bureau of Justice Statistics, National Crime Victimization Survey, 2009–2012.

Standard errors for appendix table 5: Level of distress, relationship problems, and school or work problems experienced by violent crime victims, by victim characteristics, 2009–2012

Victim characteristic	Distress				Family/friend relationship problems	Work/school problems
	No	Mild	Moderate	Severe		
Sex						
Male	1.6%	1.7%	1.4%	1.3%	1.1%	1.0%
Female	0.9	1.5	1.6	1.9	1.7	1.5
Race/Hispanic origin						
White	1.2%	1.5%	1.4%	1.5%	1.3%	1.2%
Black	2.1	2.4	2.1	2.5	2.2	1.9
Hispanic	2.1	2.6	2.2	2.4	2.0	2.0
Other	3.1	3.2	2.9	3.4	3.0	2.9
Age						
12–17	2.0%	2.5%	2.3%	1.8%	1.9%	2.2%
18–34	1.5	1.8	1.5	1.6	1.5	1.4
35–54	1.5	1.7	1.7	2.1	1.7	1.5
55 or older	2.1	2.5	2.6	3.0	2.4	1.8
Marital status						
Single, never married	1.3%	1.7%	1.5%	1.5%	1.3%	1.3%
Married	1.8	2.0	2.0	1.9	1.7	1.3
Widowed	4.4	4.3	4.9	6.8	6.0	5.6
Divorced or separated	1.7	1.8	1.8	2.5	2.1	1.9
Education						
Less than high school	2.1%	2.7%	2.6%	2.1%	2.3%	2.5%
High school degree or equivalent	1.5	1.7	1.5	1.8	1.5	1.3
College degree	1.4	1.6	1.5	1.7	1.4	1.3

Source: Bureau of Justice Statistics, National Crime Victimization Survey, 2009–2012.

Level of distress, relationship problems, and school or work problems experienced by violent crime victims, by household characteristics, 2009–2012

Household characteristic	Total	Distress				Family/friend relationship problems[a]	Work/school problems[b]
		No	Mild	Moderate	Severe		
Composition							
Single male							
No children	100%	32%	27%	16%	24%	15%	12%
With children	100%	30	26	19	25	25	20
Single female							
No children	100%	5%	21%	23%	50%	31%	24%
With children	100%	10	27	24	39	29	25
Married[c]							
No children	100%	21%	25%	24%	30%	17%	9%
With children	100%	21	32	26	21	17	14
Other[d]	100%	20	30	23	26	21	18
Income							
$24,999 or less	100%	16%	24%	23%	36%	28%	19%
$25,000–49,999	100%	23	28	23	26	19	17
$50,000–74,999	100%	19	33	27	21	15	18
$75,000 or more	100%	23	31	27	18	17	16
Unknown	100%	18	29	19	34	22	18
Location of residence							
Urban	100%	19%	28%	22%	30%	20%	16%
Suburban	100%	20	29	23	27	19	19
Rural	100%	16	28	24	31	31	18

Note: See appendix table 8 for standard errors.

[a]Includes victims reporting significant problems with family members or friends, including getting into more arguments or fights than before, not feeling able to trust them as much, or not feeling as close to them as before the crime.

[b]Includes victims reporting significant problems with job or school, such as trouble with a boss, coworker, or peer.

[c]Includes a married couple living with no other adults.

[d]Includes both single and married adults living with other adults (relatives or nonrelatives), both with and without children.

Source: Bureau of Justice Statistics, National Crime Victimization Survey, 2009–2012.

Standard errors for appendix 7: Level of distress, relationship problems, and school or work problems experienced by violent crime victims, by household characteristics, 2009–2012

Household characteristic	Distress				Family/friend relationship problems	Work/school problems
	No	Mild	Moderate	Severe		
Composition						
Single male						
No children	3.0%	2.8%	2.2%	2.7%	2.1%	1.9%
With children	5.4	5.1	4.5	5.1	5.1	4.6
Single female						
No children	1.3%	2.8%	2.9%	3.7%	3.3%	2.9%
With children	1.5	2.5	2.4	2.8	2.5	2.4
Married adults						
No children	2.7%	2.9%	2.9%	3.1%	2.4%	1.8%
With children	2.1	2.5	2.3	2.1	1.9	1.7
Other	1.4	1.7	1.5	1.6	1.5	1.4
Income						
$24,999 or less	1.5%	1.8%	1.8%	2.1%	1.9%	1.6%
$25,000–49,999	2.0	2.2	2.0	2.1	1.9	1.8
$50,000–74,999	2.2	2.8	2.6	2.3	2.0	2.2
$75,000 or more	2.1	2.4	2.3	1.9	1.8	1.8
Unknown	1.7	2.1	1.7	2.2	1.8	1.7
Location of residence						
Urban	1.4%	1.7%	1.5%	1.8%	1.5%	1.3%
Suburban	1.4	1.7	1.5	1.6	1.4	1.4
Rural	2.0	2.5	2.4	2.6	2.6	2.0

Source: Bureau of Justice Statistics, National Crime Victimization Survey, 2009–2012.

APPENDIX TABLE 9

Estimates and standard errors for figure 1: Violent crime victims who reported the crime to police or received victim services, by level of distress experienced, 2009–2012

	Estimates				Standard errors			
	No distress	Mild distress	Moderate distress	Severe distress	No distress	Mild distress	Moderate distress	Severe distress
No police or victim services	62%	59%	49%	34%	2.6%	2.3%	2.4%	2.1%
Reported to police	36	35	42	50	2.4	2.1	2.4	2.3
Received victim services	1 !	2	4	4	0.4	0.5	0.8	0.7
Both	1	4	4	12	0.4	0.7	0.7	1.3

! Interpret with caution. Estimate based on 10 or fewer sample cases, or coefficient of variation is greater than 50%.

Source: Bureau of Justice Statistics, National Crime Victimization Survey, 2009–2012.

APPENDIX TABLE 10

Estimates and standard errors for figure 2: Level of distress experienced by violent crime victims, by type of problems experienced as a result of the victimization, 2009–2012

		Estimates				Standard errors			
	Total	No distress	Mild distress	Moderate distress	Severe distress	No distress	Mild distress	Moderate distress	Severe distress
Relationship problems	100%	3%	18%	29%	51%	0.8%	2.2%	2.7%	3.1%
Problems with work/school	100%	3	16	38	42	1.0	2.4	3.4	3.5
Both	100%	4	8	23	65	1.0	1.5	2.6	3.2
Neither	100%	26	34	21	19	1.4	1.6	1.2	1.2

Source: Bureau of Justice Statistics, National Crime Victimization Survey, 2009–2012.

APPENDIX TABLE 11

Estimates and standard errors for figure 3: Level of distress experienced by violent crime victims, by type of crime, 2009–2012

		Estimates				Standard errors			
	Total	No distress	Mild distress	Moderate distress	Severe distress	No distress	Mild distress	Moderate distress	Severe distress
Total[a]									
Rape or sexual assault	100%	11%	18%	25%	46%	2.2%	2.7%	3.2%	3.8%
Robbery	100%	11	18	28	42	1.7	2.2	2.7	3.1
Aggravated assault	100%	15	28	22	35	1.7	2.3	2.1	2.5
Simple assault	100%	22	31	22	24	1.3	1.5	1.3	1.3
Completed[b]									
Rape or sexual assault	100%	10% !	21%	24%	43%	2.6%	3.7%	4.0%	4.7%
Robbery	100%	9	16	25	50	1.7	2.4	2.9	3.6
Aggravated assault	100%	8	23	22	46	1.8	2.9	2.9	3.6
Simple assault	100%	18	32	24	25	1.4	1.8	1.6	1.6

Note: Excludes victimizations in which the level of distress was unknown.

! Interpret with caution. Estimate based on 10 or fewer sample cases, or coefficient of variation is greater than 50%.

[a]Includes both threats or attempts and completed crimes.

[b]Includes only completed crimes.

Source: Bureau of Justice Statistics, National Crime Victimization Survey, 2009-2012

APPENDIX TABLE 12

Estimates and standard errors for figure 4: Level of distress experienced by serious violent crime victims, by victim–offender relationship, 2009–2012

		Estimates				Standard errors			
Type of violent crime	Total	No distress	Mild distress	Moderate distress	Severe distress	No distress	Mild distress	Moderate distress	Severe distress
Intimate partner	100%	7%	15%	19%	60%	1.8%	2.7%	3.1%	4.2%
Relative	100%	4 !	11	20	65	2.0	3.4	4.5	5.7
Other known	100%	11	24	29	36	1.8	2.6	2.8	3.1
Stranger	100%	17	27	25	31	1.9	2.4	2.3	2.5

Note: Excludes between 7% and 12% of victimizations in which the level of distress was unknown.

! Interpret with caution. Estimate based on 10 or fewer sample cases, or coeffient of variation is greater than 50%.

Source: Bureau of Justice Statistics, National Crime Victimization Survey, 2009–2012.

APPENDIX TABLE 13
Standard errors for table 1: Physical and emotional symptoms suffered by violent crime victims who experienced socio-emotional problems as a result of the victimization, by type of crime and victim–offender relationship, 2009–2012

Symptom	Type of crime			Victim–offender relationship		
	Total violence	Serious violence	Simple assault	Intimate partner	Other known	Stranger
Emotional	1.1%	1.0%	1.5%	1.7%	1.4%	1.7%
Worried or anxious	1.7	2.1	2.0	2.5	2.2	2.6
Angry	1.7	2.2	2.0	2.7	2.3	2.6
Unsafe	1.8	2.3	2.0	2.8	2.4	2.6
Violated	1.8	2.3	2.1	2.7	2.4	2.7
Vulnerable	1.8	2.4	2.1	2.8	2.4	2.7
Distrustful	1.8	2.4	2.0	2.9	2.4	2.7
Sad or depressed	1.8	2.4	2.0	2.7	2.4	2.5
Other	1.0	1.4	1.1	1.8	1.3	1.7
Physical	1.8%	2.4%	2.1%	2.7%	2.4%	2.7%
Trouble sleeping	1.8	2.4	2.0	2.9	2.4	2.5
Fatigue	1.7	2.3	1.8	3.0	2.2	2.1
Upset stomach	1.6	2.2	1.8	2.9	2.1	2.1
Muscle tension	1.6	2.2	1.7	2.8	2.1	2.2
Headaches	1.6	2.3	1.6	2.8	2.1	2.1
Problems with eating/drinking	1.5	2.2	1.6	2.9	2.0	1.8
High blood pressure	1.1	1.6	1.3	2.0	1.6	1.4
Other	0.9	1.4	0.9	1.7	1.1	1.2

Source: Bureau of Justice Statistics, National Crime Victimization Survey, 2009–2012.

APPENDIX TABLE 14
Standard errors for table 2: Victims who experienced socio-emotional problems as a result of the violent victimization, by type of crime and victim–offender relationship, 2009–2012

Type of violent crime	Total violence	Intimate partner	Other known	Stranger
Total	1.6%	2.1%	2.0%	2.0%
Serious violence	2.1%	3.2%	2.7%	2.8%
Rape or sexual assault	3.4	5.2	4.1	7.3
Robbery	2.9	6.0	3.4	3.8
Aggravated assault	2.7	4.1	3.8	3.5
Simple assault	1.7%	2.2%	2.2%	2.0%
Violence involving a weapon	2.5%	4.1%	3.6%	3.2%
Firearm	3.4	6.1	5.8	4.2
Violence involving an injury	2.2%	2.5%	2.9%	3.3%
Medical treatment received	2.6	2.5	3.8	4.0

Source: Bureau of Justice Statistics, National Crime Victimization Survey, 2009–2012.

APPENDIX TABLE 15
Standard errors for table 3: Victims who did and did not experience socio-emotional problems as a result of the violent victimization, by type of crime, 2009–2012

Type of violent crime	No socio-emotional problems	Socio-emotional problems
Serious violence	1.9%	2.1%
Rape or sexual assault	3.2	3.4
With injury	3.2	3.6
With weapon	10.1	10.2
Both injury and weapon	9.0	9.2
Without injury or weapon	4.6	4.9
Robbery	2.6	2.9
With injury	4.8	5.0
With weapon	4.2	4.5
Both injury and weapon	4.5	4.9
Without injury or weapon	4.2	4.4
Aggravated assault	2.5	2.7
With injury	4.4	4.8
With weapon	3.2	3.2
Both injury and weapon	3.7	4.0
Simple assault	1.7%	1.7%

Source: Bureau of Justice Statistics, National Crime Victimization Survey, 2009–2012.

Standard errors for table 4: Victims who experienced socio-emotional problems as a result of violent crime victimization, by location of crime and victim–offender relationship, 2009–2012

Location	Total violence	Intimate partner	Other known	Stranger
Total violence	1.6%	2.1%	2.0%	2.0%
Victim's home or lodging	2.1	2.3	3.1	5.0
Near victim's home	2.7	4.8	3.5	3.9
In, at, or near a friend, neighbor, or relative's home	3.5	6.1	4.3	5.7
Commerical place, parking lot, or other public area	2.2	4.5	3.6	2.4
School	3.0	~	3.5	4.6
Other location	2.8	5.8	4.2	3.2

~Not applicable.

Source: Bureau of Justice Statistics, National Crime Victimization Survey, 2009–2012.

Standard errors for table 5: Violent crime victims who experienced socio-emotional problems and reported the crime to police or received victim services, by victim–offender relationship, 2009–2012

	Total violence		Intimate partner		Other known		Stranger	
	No socio-emotional problems	Socio-emotional problems	No socio-emotional problems	Socio-emotional problems	No socio-emotional problems	Socio-emotional problems	No socio-emotional problems	Socio-emotional problems
Reported to police	1.9%	1.8%	5.6%	2.9%	2.5%	2.4%	2.4%	2.7%
Received victim services	0.6	1.0	3.0	2.4	1.2	1.3	0.6	0.8
Neither	2.0	1.8	5.5	2.7	2.7	2.4	2.5	2.6

Source: Bureau of Justice Statistics, National Crime Victimization Survey, 2009–2012.

Standard errors for table 6: Characteristics of violent crime victims who experienced socio-emotional problems as a result of the victimization, by type of crime, 2009–2012

Victim characteristic	Total violence	Serious violence				Simple assault
		Total	Rape or sexual assault	Robbery	Aggravated assault	
Sex						
Male	1.8%	2.7%	7.7%	3.6%	3.3%	1.9%
Female	1.8	2.3	3.4	3.6	3.2	2.0
Race/Hispanic origin						
White	1.8%	2.5%	3.7%	3.6%	3.2%	1.9%
Black	2.9	3.6	9.2	4.4	4.8	3.3
Hispanic	2.9	4.0	9.2	6.0	5.2	3.2
Other	3.9	5.4	10.0	8.6	7.1	4.5
Age						
12–17	2.7%	4.0%	8.2%	5.6%	5.4%	2.9%
18–34	2.0	2.7	4.5	4.0	3.5	2.2
35–54	2.2	3.0	5.1	4.5	4.0	2.4
55 or older	3.1	4.5	9.6	6.0	6.5	3.3
Marital status						
Single, never married	1.9%	2.5%	4.5%	3.6%	3.2%	2.0%
Married	2.4	3.6	5.2	5.6	4.6	2.6
Widowed	6.1	6.1	~	6.8	13.4	7.5
Divorced or separated	2.4	3.2	5.6	4.5	4.5	2.7
Education						
Less than high school	3.0%	4.2%	9.1%	5.7%	5.6%	3.3%
High school degree or equivalent	2.1	2.7	5.3	3.8	3.5	2.2
College degree	2.0	2.7	4.0	4.2	3.6	2.1

~Not applicable.
Source: Bureau of Justice Statistics, National Crime Victimization Survey, 2009–2012.

Standard errors for table 7: Characteristics of violent crime victims who experienced socio-emotional problems as a result of the victimization, by victim–offender relationship, 2009–2012

Victim characteristic	Intimate partner	Other known	Stranger
Sex			
Male	4.8%	2.6%	2.1%
Female	2.0	2.4	2.9
Race/Hispanic origin			
White	2.2%	2.3%	2.3%
Black	4.4	4.0	4.0
Hispanic	6.0	4.2	3.7
Other	6.8	5.8	5.0
Age			
12–17	~	3.2%	3.9%
18–34	2.9%	2.9	2.6
35–54	2.5	3.1	3.0
55 or older	5.5	3.7	4.4
Marital status			
Single, never married	3.1%	2.5%	2.4%
Married	4.7	3.2	3.0
Widowed	~	6.4	10.0
Divorced or separated	2.4	3.6	3.7
Education			
Less than high school	~	3.5%	4.7%
High school degree or equivalent	3.3%	2.8	2.7
College degree	2.3	2.7	2.5

~Not applicable.

Source: Bureau of Justice Statistics, National Crime Victimization Survey, 2009–2012.

Standard errors for table 8: Household characteristics of violent crime victims who experienced socio-emotional problems as a result of the victimization, by type of crime, 2009–2012

Household characteristics	Total violence	Serious violence				Simple assault
		Total	Rape or sexual assault	Robbery	Aggravated assault	
Composition						
Single male						
No children	3.3%	4.8%	9.9%	6.7%	6.2%	3 5%
With children	6.1	9.3	23.1	~	10.7	6 8
Single female						
No children	3.1	4.2	6.2	4.8	7.1	4 1
With children	2.8	3.6	5.2	5.4	5.1	2 8
Married						
No children	3.6	5.6	8.1	8.9	7.7	3 8
With children	2.8	4.4	7.9	7.9	5.4	3 0
Other	2.0	2.7	4.9	3.8	3.5	2 1
Income						
$24,999 or less	2.2%	2.9%	5.8%	3.7%	3.9%	2 6%
$25,000–49,999	2.6	3.7	7.1	6.2	4.4	2 8
$50,000–74,999	3.1	4.4	5.2	8.0	6.5	3 3
$75,000 or more	2.7	4.3	7.2	6.9	5.5	2 8
Unknown	2.4	3.3	6.8	4.5	4.6	2 6
Location of residence						
Urban	2.0%	2.7%	5.2%	3.6%	3.5%	2 2%
Suburban	2.0	2.8	4.1	4.1	3.7	2 1
Rural	2.9	4.4	8.7	7.0	5.5	3 1

~Not applicable.

Source: Bureau of Justice Statistics, National Crime Victimization Survey, 2009–2012.

Standard errors for table 9: Household characteristics of violent crime victims who experienced socio-emotional problems as a result of the victimization, by victim–offender relationship, 2009–2012

Household characteristic	Intimate partner	Other known	Stranger
Composition			
Single male			
No children	7.8%	4.9%	4.1%
With children	5.3	9.4	7.7
Single female			
No children	3.1	4.4	5.0
With children	3.0	4.1	5.0
Married			
No children	6.9	4.6	4.5
With children	7.3	3.6	3.8
Other	2.8	2.7	2.5
Income			
$24,999 or less	3.1%	2.9%	3.3%
$25,000–49,999	4.2	3.6	3.3
$50,000–74,999	5.3	4.4	3.9
$75,000 or more	2.4	3.9	3.2
Unknown	3.5	3.3	3.4
Location of residence			
Urban	2.9%	2.9%	2.6%
Suburban	2.8	2.6	2.6
Rural	4.0	3.7	4.8

Source: Bureau of Justice Statistics, National Crime Victimization Survey, 2009–2012.

Coefficients and standard errors for table 10: Logistic regression analysis of the effect of victim characteristics, type of crime, and victim–offender relationship on the probability of victims experiencing socio-emotional problems, 2009–2012

	First model		Final model	
	B	Standard error	B	Standard error
Victim characteristic				
Female	0.93	0.10	0.97	0.10
Black	-0.19	0.15	~	~
Other race	-0.02	0.22	~	~
Hispanic	-0.08	0.17	~	~
Ages 18–34	-0.13	0.15	~	~
Ages 35–54	0.37	0.16	0.42	0.11
Age 55 or older	0.66	0.18	0.76	0.13
Married	-0.05	0.13	~	~
Widowed	0.13	0.33	~	~
Divorced or separated	-0.03	0.14	~	~
Less than high school degree	0.41	0.26	~	~
High school degree or equivalent	-0.07	0.11	~	~
Type of crime				
Rape or sexual assault	0.59	0.28	~	~
Robbery	1.20	0.21	0.99	0.15
Aggravated assault	0.44	0.25	~	~
Victim–offender relationship				
Intimate partner	1.77	0.19	1.69	0.19
Other known	0.71	0.11	0.72	0.11
Incident characteristics				
Series victimization	-0.23	0.18	~	~
Injury	0.60	0.13	0.67	0.12
Weapon present	0.20	0.24	0.54	0.13
Do not know if weapon present	0.55	0.20	0.54	0.18

~Characteristics deleted from model when Wald statistic was not significant at the 95%-confidence level.

Source: Bureau of Justice Statistics, National Crime Victimization Survey, 2009–2012.

Standard errors for table 11: Characteristics of incidents and victims who were and were not administered NCVS distress questions, 2009–2012

Characteristic	Distress questions not administered	Distress questions administered
Type of violence		
Rape or sexual assau t	0.3%	1.0%
Robbery	0.8	1.5
Aggravated assault	1.0	1.9
Simple assault	1.4	2.6
Victim–offender relationship		
Intimate partner	0.7%	1.8%
Relative	0.4	1.2
Other known	1.3	2.5
Stranger	1.1	2.7
Sex		
Male	1.6%	2.8%
Female	1.5	2.8
Race/Hispanic origin		
White	1.6%	2.7%
Black	1.1	1.7
Hispanic	0.9	1.7
Other	0.5	1.1
Age		
12–17	1.0%	1.9%
18–34	1.5	2.7
35–54	1.4	2.4
55 or older	0.7	1.5
Income		
$24,999 or less	1.0%	2.4%
$25,000–49,999	1.1	2.0
$50,000–74,999	0.9	1.5
$75,000 or more	1.0	1.9
Unknown	1.4	2.2
Location of residence		
Urban	1.4%	2.7%
Suburban	1.6	2.7
Rural	0.9	1.7

Source: Bureau of Justice Statistics, National Crime Victimization Survey. 2008–2012

Estimates and standard errors for figure 5: Recency of interview, by level of distress reported, 2009–2012

		Estimates				Standard errors			
	Total	No distress	Mild distress	Moderate distress	Severe distress	No distress	Mild distress	Moderate distress	Severe distress
Less than a month	100%	21%	28%	25%	26%	1.9%	2.1%	2.0%	2.7%
1 month	100%	17	31	24	28	1.9	2.5	2.3	2.4
2 months	100%	16	26	25	33	1.8	2.3	2.3	2.5
3 months	100%	18	29	24	29	2.2	2.7	2.5	2.7
4 months	100%	21	31	17	31	2.2	2.6	2.0	2.6
5 months	100%	22	27	24	28	1.8	2.0	1.9	2.7

Source: Bureau of Justice Statistics, National Crime Victimization Survey 2009–2012.

www.ingramcontent.com/pod-product-compliance
Lightning Source LLC
Chambersburg PA
CBHW081545280526
45788CB00010B/3362